Rupen Das has helped us i practical and proven guide This book is one of a number of new publications that will help us break out of the Western hegemony in theological education. We will all be richer as each seminary diversifies its curriculum to suit its particular context. Das provides a tool kit that can be adapted for that purpose in each place and so demonstrates the manifold greatness of our creative God.

Stuart Brooking
Executive Director
Overseas Council Australia

In the midst of a great process for global theological education transformation, this book comes to provide the material for those that want to see schools being agents in preparing leaders and churches for contextual impact. We receive this book with great appreciation.

Josue Fernandez
Overseas Council Regional Director for Latin America and The Caribbean,
Presbítero for Asociación Vida Abundante, Tucumán, Argentina

Rupen Das has deep understanding and extensive experience in organizational processes and theological training. In this book, he has done what few people have the requisite background to do – to bring clarity to the thinking about, and the practice of, theological training by using the process and evaluative tools of Results Based Management. This is a unique and very helpful contribution to theological training. All theological educators who read this book will wish it had been available to them much earlier.

Fong Choon Sam
Dean of Academic Studies
Baptist Theological Seminary, Singapore

Succinctly, persuasively and practically this handbook presents various approaches to theological education and insists that the effectiveness of that education is evidenced by the graduate's leadership ability in the ministry context. Every seminary president and academic dean would benefit from the assessment tools within.

Harry Gardner
President, Acadia Divinity College,
Dean of Theology, Acadia University

Failure to connect with context and to assess the impact of its graduates in churches and communities have been a serious weakness in theological education. In this book, the author deals with the why and how of designing a relevant curriculum and assessing its effectiveness in the context of our students and graduates. Seminary leaders and faculty should take time to discuss it in faculty meetings and retreats and use it as a guide in making the much-needed change in their training programs.

Theresa Roco Lua
Secretary of Accreditation and Educational Development,
Asia Theological Association
Dean, Asia Graduate School of Theology, Philippines

In this engaging and readable text, Dr Rupen Das has connected his passion for the church with his commitment to quality, relevant, theological education. Sample rubrics and questionnaires, as well as a Toolkit, provide helpful models for schools to reference as they seek to develop their own contextualized rubrics for assessment. Clear communication deepens and enriches every personal encounter. In this book, Dr Das has communicated both the urgency of the task to understand and embrace the richness of the contexts in which we teach and minister, and the mandate for education to be relevant in the place where our roots run deep.

Melody Mazuk
Global Theological Librarian

All theology is contextual. In an increasingly global world, this reality has become clear to some and to others a point of contention. Rupen Das in this small book brilliantly unpacks the idea that theological education must be rooted in place. It calls us to take context seriously so that rigorous reflection emerging out of praxis can occur. This is a must read for the twenty-first-century theological institutions across the globe.

Gary V. Nelson
President
Tyndale University College & Seminary

Doesn't everyone involved in leadership development desire to be more effective in their work? If our answer is, of course!, the next question is not so simple: HOW can we become more effective in this exalting but daunting task of training leaders? Dr Rupen Das has given us a foundational response, found in the title of his new book, Connecting Curriculum with Context. This short book is so much more than a nice alliterated title with the key words beginning with C. Allow me to add a few C's to explain.

Das' book is **concise** – only eighty-six pages in length, but packed with essential, invaluable information. It is clear – so very user-friendly and readable. It is also **crucial** – because the way in which we interface our educational program with the challenges of our contexts is a key to the long-term development and sustainability of our training institutions. It is **conceptual** – setting forth and unpacking the key notions permitting us to wrap our minds around this connecting task. Lastly, this book is **concrete** – containing very practical exercises that will help us connect the understanding gained from these pages to our institutional and contextual realities.

Do read this book. It won't take much of your time. And you will not regret it.

Paul Sanders
International Director Emeritus, ICETE

ICETE Series

Connecting Curriculum with Context

ICETE International Council for Evangelical Theological Education
strengthening evangelical theological education through international cooperation

Langham
GLOBAL LIBRARY

Connecting Curriculum with Context

A Handbook for Context Relevant Curriculum Development in Theological Education

Rupen Das

Series Editor
Riad Kassis

ICETE International Council for Evangelical Theological Education
strengthening evangelical theological education through international cooperation

Langham
GLOBAL LIBRARY

© 2015 by Rupen Das

Published 2015 by Langham Global Library
an imprint of Langham Creative Projects

Langham Partnership
PO Box 296, Carlisle, Cumbria CA3 9WZ, UK
www.langham.org

ISBNs:
978-1-78368-068-9 Print
978-1-78368-070-2 Mobi
978-1-78368-069-6 ePub
978-1-78368-071-9 PDF

British Library Cataloguing in Publication Data
A catalogue record for this book is available from the British Library

ISBN: 978-1-78368-068-9

Cover & Book Design: projectluz.com

Contents

Foreword xi

Acknowledgements. xiii

1   **Introduction: The Challenge of Context** 1
      1. Background 1
      2. The Problem. 2
      3. Context, Theology and Theological Training 3
      4. Models of Training 10
      5. Theological Training and Need 18
      6. Exercises 20

2   **Understanding Effectiveness** 23
      1. Organizational Theory 23
      2. Organizational Capacity Assessment 25
      3. Exercise 28

3   **Connecting Curriculum with Context** 39
      1. Understanding the Connection of Curriculum to Context. 40
      2. Designing a Feedback Mechanism 44
      3. Frequency and Methods of Assessments 48
      4. Assessing Effectiveness 51
      5. Exercise - Organizing the Process. 54

4   **Managing Change and Being an Agent of Change** 57
      1. Managing the Process of Change 58
      2. Being an Agent of Change 60

Appendix: Sample Toolkit 65

Bibliography 71

Foreword

I wholeheartedly believe that theological education should be in the service of the church. Its major, but not only, goal is to contribute effectively to the growth and development of the local and global church. In 2012, the International Council for Evangelical Theological Education (ICETE) had its triennial global consultation in Nairobi, Kenya. The theme of the consultation was "Rooted in the Word. Engaged in the World." However, even when we are truly deeply rooted in God's Word and fully engaged with our context, how do we know that our theological training programs are effective and contributing to the growth of the church? Is it possible to measure and assess the outcome and impact of theological education on both church and society? How does such assessment influence our curricula and learning methods? What are the practical ways to connect our curriculum with our social, political, and religious contexts?

In this book, Dr Rupen Das skillfully addresses these significant questions. He does this with strong passion for the church, deep insights from the world of theological education, and by providing down to earth practicalities. Indian wisdom has left its imprint on Dr Das, enabling him to be eloquent and concise in addressing the whole issue of outcome and impact-based assessment in theological training.

This book is not a theoretical work, although its implications are based on solid theory of education and non-profit management principles. It presents efficient tools for the renewal of theological education. It is a well-known fact that theological training worldwide invests substantial human and financial resources to train pastors, preachers, teachers and other Christian leaders for the work of the kingdom. Therefore, this book will be enthusiastically welcomed by theological educators, church leaders and funding agencies alike.

The launch of this book coincides providentially as well as intentionally with the ICETE triennial global consultation that will be dealing with the very theme of outcome and impact-based assessment of theological training. It gives me great pleasure to recommend this book to all who are involved in such a noble task. It is my hope and prayer that by the application of the principles and tools outlined in this book that we bring all glory and honor to our Triune God.

Rev Riad Kassis, PhD
International Director, ICETE
Director, Langham Scholars Ministry, Langham Partnership

Acknowledgements

The genesis of this idea was in a conversation with Gordon King, a colleague at Canadian Baptist Ministries (CBM). CBM provides funding for development and relief projects, as well as leadership development and theological training. Internationally accepted systems for planning and evaluating relief and development projects were already in place, tools such as Results Based Management (RBM). The question that Gordon asked was if it was possible to adapt these tools and processes of thinking to evaluate the effectiveness of theological training. The questions led to a series of discussions within CBM with colleagues such as Terry Smith, Sam Chaise and Colin Godwin, among others, as to how this could be done. It culminated in a workshop hosted by the Arab Baptist Theological Seminary (ABTS) in Beirut, Lebanon, where CBM brought together its entire global staff involved in theological education to explore this concept further.

It was at this workshop that another of my colleagues, Elie Haddad, the President of ABTS, decided to pilot the concept at ABTS. The two issues were: how effectively does ABTS's curriculum connect with the contexts where its graduates minister, and how would ABTS assess its effectiveness as a theological training institution. Stuart Brooking at Overseas Council Australia (OCA) liked the idea and provided funding for the pilot project to develop the assessment tools and conduct the first round of assessments. Greg Matthews, at that time an intern with ABTS, lead the field research, collated the data and provided the initial report, as well as helping modify the assessment tools. Rosette Mansour was involved in arranging some of the field logistics for meetings with ATBS graduates.

The pilot project had a reference board that met to review the thinking and the work that had been done and provide feedback. This included Stuart Brooking, Scott Cunningham, Riad Kassis, Ashish Chrispal, Melody Mazuk and Sam Barkat. The concept was then presented and tested at various Overseas Council International (OCI) trainings and Institutes. Perry Shaw at ABTS has been another good colleague, whose own pioneering work on curriculum development dovetailed with what was being attempted here. Others who were involved in conversations at various points and whose insights were helpful were Marvin Oxenham and Paul Clark.

I cannot underestimate the influence on my thinking of the doctoral thesis of my friend, Teemu Lehtonen, in which he researched theological education in a global context. His thoughts and research are reflected in chapter 1 in ways that I have not been able to fully cite. Nishant Das helped in making the diagrams used in the book look presentable and understandable, and Layla Ho was invaluable with editing this to make it readable.

There is an anonymous saying: "Success has many fathers, while failure is an orphan." All the people mentioned above and many more have contributed to where this thinking on connecting curriculum with context and assessing the effectiveness of seminaries is at this point. In many ways, what is presented here is fairly obvious. After all, isn't this the way much of education should be. American writer and philosopher Walker Percy in describing his art states, ". . . you are telling the reader or listener or the viewer something he already knows but which he doesn't quite know that he knows, so that in the act of communication he experiences a recognition, a feeling that he has been there before, a shock of recognition."[1]

Psalm 115:1 – "Not to us, LORD, not to us but to your name be the glory, because of your love and faithfulness.

Rupen Das
Amsterdam, 2015

---

1. Walker Percy, in *Conversations with Walker Percy*, ed. Peggy Whitman Prenshaw (Jackson: University of Mississippi Press, 1985), 24.

1

Introduction:
The Challenge of Context

1. Background

Educational institutions globally are under increasing scrutiny as to whether the education that they provide is relevant to the local and global communities that they serve. Some of these questions deal with the kind of return on investment students expect from the high cost they pay for post-secondary education. *The central question is whether these institutions are being responsive to increasingly volatile and fast-changing social, economic and political contexts, and pluralistic societies.*

Seminaries are not immune from these questions. Until recently, most seminaries operated on the basis of imparting a core of knowledge that comprised of the foundational truths of the Christian faith. There were additional courses on homiletics and practical theology, namely, the skills needed for pastoral practice. The curriculum was a fairly standard package that could be transported across cultures and continents and was not sensitive to local culture, traditions and values.

Some institutions have been more sensitive to context and have a graduate profile, which identified the knowledge, skills and attitudes necessary to be effective in pastoral ministry in a specific context. This profile usually provides a template for the institution to ensure that its courses and training are focused on ensuring that the necessary knowledge, skills and attitudes are acquired by the time of graduation. The profiles of some institutions also provide a framework for the graduate to continue learning over a lifetime. In some cases, the graduate profile would have been based on a formal or informal assessment of needs at a specific point in time within the churches where the graduates serve. However, most seminaries do not have a systematic and responsive mechanism that connects a changing context with the curriculum.

The issue of context raises the question as to what is the focus of seminary training. Is the focus to train the students to become pastors who are able *to do the work of the ministry* through activities such as evangelism, leading Bible studies, counseling, and preaching? Or is the focus on training the students *to enable and equip* church members to mature in Christ so that they are able to do the work of the ministry (Eph 4:12–15)? If the focus is only on the student to become a pastor, then any evaluation of effectiveness of the institution is based on whether the student completed the curriculum and was successfully trained. If the focus of training is on the graduate being able to equip a local church "for the work of ministry," then an evaluation of the effectiveness of the curriculum does not end with the student successfully graduating, but on the graduate's progress to equip the church where they minister.

While some seminaries would say that they do the latter, their courses may not reflect this. They may have courses on evangelism, discipleship, church planting, and what it means to be a missional church. But there would be little on how to equip church members to be effective in their ministries. The result is that often the pastor does all the "work of ministry" while the church members are not involved in meaningful ways. There is often little discussion on what impact on society and maturity of a congregation would actually look like (what does "attaining to the whole measure of the fullness of Christ" mean).

2. The Problem

With the volatile changes taking place in so much of the global south, there are new factors that are impacting churches. The question is whether there are leaders who can guide and shepherd congregations through these times. There is a growing need for leaders who can move beyond merely trying to protect their churches from decline and decay and see God given opportunities for ministry and for declaring the Kingdom of God. There is a need for leaders who know more than the basics of biblical truth and preaching the Word, and who are also able to address the issues in society confronting their church and its members from a biblical perspective – to be salt and light in their communities. The question of relevance is becoming increasingly important.

Part of the answer to these challenges lies in how the seminaries are responding to a changing environment. Are they asking questions about the relevance of their training and curriculum to the contexts that their graduates will be living and ministering in? These questions need to be addressed at a number of different levels:

- What theological understanding do the students need in order to understand and interpret their social, political, economic and religious contexts? While contextual theology may make some nervous because of the fear of deviating from what they understand to be the core tenets of the Christian faith, being able to develop contextual theology is critical in ensuring relevance of the revealed Word of God in a specific context.
- Do the students also have the tools for cultural exegesis and social analysis in order to understand a changing and volatile context? What implications does cultural exegesis and social analysis have for the training in practical theology, whether it is in preaching, teaching, training in discipleship or counseling?

The core of the problem is that most educational institutions (seminaries are no exception) do not realize that they operate within dynamic and complex social, economic, political and religious systems, and as a result do not have the administrative mechanisms that are able to identify changes in society and in the church and then respond accordingly, while maintaining the core of biblical truth.

3.   Context, Theology and Theological Training

It would be naïve to believe that anyone could read the Scriptures without the lenses of their own culture, gender, social and economic status, life experiences, season of life, political ideology, and value system. In order to become effective pastors, it is critical that seminary graduates understand the lenses of their church members. Trinity Lutheran Seminary professor, Mark Allan Powell, gives an example of life experiences influencing how one reads the Bible. He had his American students read the parable of the prodigal son in Luke 15:11–31, close their Bibles and then retell the story as faithfully as possible to their student partner. Powell notes that not a single one of his students mentioned the famine in Luke 15:14. Sometime later, while teaching in St Petersburg in Russia, he asked fifty participants to do the same. Forty-two of the fifty mentioned the famine. Why the difference? The Russians remembered or had been told first-hand of the Nazi siege of the city during World War II when 670,000 died from starvation. Their experience influenced how they read the Bible. Powell notes that for them, the parable was about God rescuing them from a desperate circumstance. While for the American students, who had never experienced a famine, the parable was about a disobedient son who repents and returns to his father, who in turns forgives him.

This is known as *domain specificity.* It means that a person's reactions, mode of thinking and intuition is dependent on the context in which the matter is presented. It is "what evolutionary psychologists call the 'domain' of the object or event . . . We react to a piece of information not on its logical merits, but on the basis of which framework surrounds it, and how it registers with our social-emotional system."[1]

Theology and context are integrally linked and this needs to be reflected in the training at seminaries. Princeton University theologian Daniel Migliore articulates the need to be aware of context and values. "Confession of Jesus Christ takes place in particular historical and cultural contexts. Our response to the questions of who we say Jesus Christ is and how he helps us is shaped in important ways by the particular context in which these questions arise."[2]

For a long time, theology focused on articulating the core and essence of the Christian faith systematically, referred to as "Biblical and Systematic Theology." It was believed that this constituted a corpus of truth that was not only unchangeable in the way it was articulated but was complete in and of itself. Canadian theologian Douglas John Hall describes that the challenge of Systematic Theology relating to context is in the very nature of what Systematic Theology is meant to be. He writes:

---

1. Nassim Nicholas Taleb, *The Black Swan: The Impact of the Highly Improbable* (New York: Random House Trade Paperbacks, 2010), 53.
2. Daniel Migliore, *Faith Seeking Understanding: An Introduction to Christian Theology* (Grand Rapids: Eerdmans, 2004), 197.

Systematic or dogmatic theology has been slow to learn the lessons of contextuality, especially its place-component, and one cannot avoid the conclusion that a (if not the) predominant reason for this lies in the character of the enterprise as such. The very adjectives *systematic* and *dogmatic* . . . betray a predilection to permanency. It so easily happens that a . . . desire to "see the thing whole," to integrate, to describe connections, to honor the unity of the truth, and so on becomes, in its execution, an exercise in finality.[3]

However, over time the understanding of what theology is has moved beyond this to try and understand the relevance of our faith and spirituality in an increasingly complex and pluralistic world where moral dilemmas are pushing against boundaries that have not previously existed.[4] Migliore writes about this **process**.

Theology must be *critical reflection* on the community's faith and practice. Theology is not simply reiteration of what has been or is currently believed and practiced by a community of faith . . . when this responsibility for critical reflection is neglected or relegated to a merely ornamental role, the faith of the community is invariably threatened by shallowness, arrogance and ossification.[5]

From the 1920s to the 1950s one of the things Karl Barth focused on was the **attitude** that is required as the community of faith seeks to examine itself in the light of revealed truth. "Theology is an act of repentant humility . . . This act exists in the fact that in theology the church seeks again and again to examine itself critically as it asks itself what it means and implies to be a church among men."[6]

Alister McGrath defines the **understanding of theology**. He writes that Christian theology "is therefore understood to mean the systematic study

---

3. Douglas John Hall, *The Cross in Our Context: Jesus and the Suffering World* (Minneapolis: Fortress Press, 2003), 45.
4. The Gospel and Our Culture Network, http://www.gocn.org/ is "A network to provide useful research regarding the encounter between the gospel and our culture, and to encourage local action for transformation in the life and witness of the church."
5. Migliore, *Faith Seeking Understanding*, xv.
6. Karl Barth, *God in Action* (Edinburgh: T & T. Clark, 1936), 44.

of the ideas of the Christian faith"[7] which include the issues of sources, of development, of relationships, and of applications.[8] With specific regards to applications he says, "Christian theology is not just a set of ideas: it is about making possible a new way of seeing ourselves, others, and the world, with implications for the way in which we behave."[9]

So while truth is universal, theology is contextual because it influences how we live out our faith and spirituality. Most of the basic understandings in systematic theology evolved and crystalized as a result of questions or challenges to the Christian faith during specific periods of history. So in effect, all theology is contextual. For example, John Calvin's *Institutes of the Christian Religion* are his **theological method**. Though Martin Luther and Huldrych Zwingli wrote extensively, they never systematized their theology. Calvin's *Institutes* is one of the earliest major systematic presentations of the core of Reformation theology. In retrospect, the *Institutes* are a reflection of Calvin's attempts at developing theology in the context of sixteenth-century Europe, and then applying theology to daily life, specifically in Geneva. For Calvin, theology was not just an academic discipline developed in isolation, but it was developed and applied in context.

Gustavo Gutierrez, the Peruvian theologian and Dominican priest, often referred to as the voice of Liberation Theology, states the obvious:

> People today often talk about contextual theologies but, in point
> of fact, theology has always been contextual . . . When Augustine
> wrote *The City of God*, he was reflecting on what it meant for him
> and for his contemporaries to live the gospel within a specific
> context of serious historical transformations.[10]

---

7. Alister E. McGrath, *Christian Theology: An Introduction.* 5th. (Chichester: Wiley-Blackwell, 2011), 101.
8. The "sources" address the sources on which Christian ideas are based and include the Christian Bible, tradition, reason and experience. "Development" looks at how ideas have evolved over time. This is the field of historical theology. "Relationships" looks at how the various Christian ideas relate to each other – "the interconnected network of ideas". McGrath, *Christian Theology*, 101.
9. Ibid., 102.
10. Daniel Hartnett, "Remembering the Poor: An Interview with Gustavo Gutierrez," *America, the National Catholic Weekly* (2003), 3 February, accessed 14 December 2010, http://www.americamagazine.org/content/article.cfm?article_id=2755.

Yale Divinity School theologian, Hans Frei's *Typologies of Christian Theology*[11] describes the spectrum of **theological engagement with specific contexts**. On one end of the spectrum is theology as a unique academic discipline (and not necessarily Christian), which is universal in its content and has no specific relationship with context, if any. On the other end of the spectrum is Christian self-description (different from academic theology). This defines itself solely from Scripture and Christian experience, which is usually influenced significantly by personal experience, context and culture.

Hans Frei's colleague at Yale, Richard Niebuhr's taxonomy on *Christ and Culture* elaborates on engagement with context.[12] The understanding of how Christ relates to culture has a profound impact on the content of theological training curriculum to ensure relevance of content to culture. His taxonomy consists of five categories:

- *Christ against Culture* – This is based on 1 John as well as John 2:15–17 and 5:5, where the world is understood as the society that is outside the church. Niebuhr writes that in this category, "The counterpart of loyalty to Christ and the brothers is the rejection of cultural society."[13]
- *Christ of Culture* – Christ is seen as the pinnacle of human achievement. Niebuhr writes, "In every culture to which the gospel comes there are men who hail Jesus as the Messiah of their society, the fulfiller of its hopes and aspiration."[14] A pioneer in this thinking was Bishop John Nicol Farquhar in India whose book in 1913 entitled *The Crown of Hinduism* focused on the theology of "fulfillment," in that Christ not only came to fulfill the law and the prophets (Matt 5:17) but also all the world's "higher religions." It is in this sense that he stated that Christ is the "crown" of Hinduism.
- *Christ above Culture* – In Matthew 22:21 Jesus exhorts his disciples "to render to Caesar the things that are Caesar's, and to God the things that are God's." So according to Niebuhr, there is the realm where we live amidst culture, and the realm where Christ is. So

---

11. Hans W. Frei, *Types of Christian Theology*, eds. George Hunsinger and William C. Plancher (New Haven: Yale University Press, 1992).
12. H. Richard Niebuhr, *Christ and Culture* (New York: Harper, 1951).
13. Ibid., 47.
14. Ibid., 83.

culture is separate from Christ. Niebuhr writes, "The synthesist alone seems to provide for willing and intelligent cooperation with non-believers in carrying on the work of the world, while yet maintaining the distinctiveness of Christian faith and life."[15]

- *Christ and Culture in Paradox* – The believer and the world exist in tension. The starting point of dealing with any cultural problem must be God's act of reconciliation through Christ. The believer who lives in this duality and tension "knows he belongs to the culture and cannot get out of it, that God indeed sustains him in it and by it."[16]
- *Christ the Transformer of Culture* – While there is a profound influence of sin upon the world, Niebuhr recognizes Christ as the redeemer. Niebuhr agrees with the theology of Augustine who saw Christ as the transformer of culture, the Christ who "redirects, reinvigorates and regenerates that life of man, expressed in all human works."[17]

Baptist theologian and ethicist James McClendon elaborates on the concept of theological engagement with specific contexts. He states that there are two facts that undergird the development of theology and Christian ethics. The first of these is that theology is not without hard struggles. This struggle is seen in the interaction between the world and the theology held by the church. He states that theology, which is the basic points of view of the church, and the perspective of the world, are not the same. He writes, "The church's story will not interpret the world to the world's satisfaction."[18] This difference cannot be diminished. He explains, "Conspiring to conceal the difference between the church and the world, we may in the short run entice the world, but we will only do so by betraying the world."[19]

The reason theology will always struggle with the world is because there is a moral dimension rooted in a biblical worldview in theology's interaction with culture. The gospel will always confront the evil in culture and society. Veteran missionary and missiologist Paul Heibert warns that contextualization is not an indiscriminate adopting of culture, customs and values:

15. Ibid., 143.
16. Ibid., 156.
17. Ibid., 209.
18. James McClendon, *Ethics: Systematic Theology Vol. 1*, (Nashville: Abingdon Press, 2002), 17.
19. Ibid., 18.

The foreignness of the culture we add to the gospel offends and must be eliminated. But the gospel itself offends. It is supposed to offend, and we dare not weaken its offense. The gospel must be contextualized but it must remain prophetic. It must stand in judgment of what is evil in all cultures as well as in all persons.[20]

Therefore attaining the right balance in interacting with the world is a challenge. Mennonite theologian Thomas Finger states that the church cannot be separated from the world, though, as he states, the Anabaptists have sometimes attempted to do this. Finger writes, "Theology is always in dialogue with its cultural contexts . . . including the academic sphere. Theology tests the church's current beliefs and often revises them through conversations with its culture. Anabaptists should not only celebrate their distinctives but also recognize how preoccupation with distinctives can encourage narrowness, exclusivity and a false sense of superiority."[21]

The second fact McClendon states is that because the church is not one congruent whole, there are divided theologies. He refers to German theologian Friedrich Schleiermacher, whom he considers the father of modern theology, who argued that any given theology must represent and refer to the doctrine of some particular Christian body at a particular time.[22] So the various theological approaches and streams arise from specific contexts at specific times, which may or may not be relevant in other contexts in different periods of history.

British theologian and missiologist Andrew Walls refers to the "translation principle," when the gospel, the Good News of Jesus Christ, is communicated in different cultures and places. Walls writes, "Incarnation is translation. When God in Christ became man, divinity was translated into humanity . . . The first divine act of translation thus gives rise to a constant succession of new translations. Christian diversity is the necessary product of the incarnation." While this translation includes language and culture, one wonders if it should also include patterns of thought and reasoning, as well as philosophical frameworks and worldviews. While the gospel message

---

20. Paul Heibert, *Anthropological Reflections on Missiological Issues* (Grand Rapids: Baker, 1994), 86.
21. Thomas N. Finger, *Contemporary Anabaptist Theology: Biblical, Historical, Constructive* (Downers Grove: InterVarsity Press, 2004), 96.
22. McClendon, *Ethics,* 18.

is universal, it is contextual in the way it is translated and understood in different cultures and socio-economic groups.

Theology needs to be systematic, but it also needs to be relevant in each and every context where the church is present. Contextualization will always result in the gospel standing in judgment of society and therefore there needs to be critical reflection by the church on what God has to say about issues of injustice, social concern, traditions, culture, and values in a specific context. The local church does not exist in a vacuum, separate from society, but is an institution in the community. Douglas John Hall points out that a focus on a single systematic and dogmatic theology in its "reluctance to open itself to the great *variety* of worldly contexts . . . has again and again resisted criticism from the perspectives of those whose worlds were virtually ignored or excluded in the great systems of Christian thought. This is not a mere academic concern, for the excluded ones have not just been individuals, or tiny minorities, but whole populations, whole races, whole economic and other groupings."[23] *Any Christian ministry or Christian ethic and the church's response to social issues need to flow out of the understanding of contextual theology.*

Theological training ultimately is meant to train individuals to minister in specific contexts. Eugene Peterson writes as a pastor, that all theology is rooted in geography. "Now is the time to rediscover the meaning of the local, and in terms of church, the parish. All churches are local. All pastoral work takes place geographically."[24] If this is true, then do the graduates have the ability and the tools to understand the local?

4. Models of Training

The effectiveness of the type of training for Christian vocation is directly connected to the context within which the graduates will be ministering. While distinctions are made between the types of training provided by a Bible school, a seminary, and the theology department of a university, these categories with their courses and graduation requirements are in no way standardized and the categories are not discrete.

---

23. Hall, *The Cross*, 48.
24. Eugene Peterson, *Under the Unpredictable Plant: An Exploration in Vocational Holiness* (Grand Rapids: Eerdmans Publishing, 1994), 128.

There are three commonly accepted models of theological education. The original thinking was developed by David Kelsey of Yale Divinity School as a bipolar approach of **classical** versus **vocational**, reflecting "the two normative types of theological education."[25] To this was added Robert Bank's **missional** approach.[26]

The classical model, sometimes referred to as "Athens," defines theological education as Christian character formation or *paideia* (παιδεία). It is derived from classical Greek philosophical educational methodology and literally means child rearing or education, and is a process of molding character. It was a system of cultural education for older children that included rhetoric, grammar, mathematics, music, philosophy, natural history, and gymnastics – all the subjects that were valued in ancient Greek culture. The objective was to produce well-rounded and fully educated citizens.[27] The concept of *paideia* does not start with the individual person and their potential but with the concept of the ideal person. So the process of education was to educate and mold human beings into the ideal man who represented human nature in its truest form. Philosophers, artists, sculptors, educators and poets drew their inspiration from the concept of an ideal man. The goal of classical education was the transformation of the individual.

The early church adopted and then adapted this model. Some of the church Fathers saw the Christian faith as a form of *paideia,* that in order to grow in one's faith, one's character had to be formed. By the medieval and monastic period it had become the dominant educational philosophy. For Gregory of Nyssa the goal of Christianity was *deificatio* (Latin, meaning "making divine" or edification), and *paideia* (character formation and molding worldview) was the way to achieve it. *Paideia* also influenced Basil of Caesarea in the development of his monastic rules.[28] The objective was to enable individuals to develop a holistic vision that understands and grasps the totality of life, including the world. Rather than just knowing about God, the focus was on

25. David H. Kelsey, *Between Athens and Berlin: The Theological Debate* (Grand Rapids: Eerdmans, 1993), 27.
26. Robert Banks, *Reenvisioning Theological Education* (Grand Rapids: Eerdmans, 1999).
27. Richard Tarnas, *The Passion of the Western Mind: Understanding the Ideas that Have Shaped Our World View* (New York: Harmony Books, 1993), 29–30.
28. Werner Jaeger, *Early Christianity and Greek Paideia* (Cambridge: Harvard University Press, 1961), 90. St. Basil's *Wider and Shorter Rules* became the model for eastern monasticism from the 5th century onward. They influenced the development of the monastic orders established by St Benedict of Norcia, St Dominic, and St Francis of Assisi.

knowing God. Brian Edgar at Asbury Theological Seminary writes, "It is not about *theology*, that is, the formal study of the *knowledge* of God, but it is more about what Kelsey calls *theologia,* that is gaining the wisdom of God."[29] The emphasis was on holiness and the transformation of the individual. Edgar states that in this model of theological education, holiness, and moral and spiritual transformation are central. He states that the implication is that curriculum needs to address the issues of personal and moral formation of the student, and the values of the faculty and institution need to be aligned in a way to accomplish that.

The vocational model, referred to as "Berlin" and with its roots in the Enlightenment, sees theological education as being a preparation for a professional Christian vocation and therefore needed to be situated within the context of a university as an academic discipline. The term *wissenschaft* is a German term that means a study or science that requires systematic research. The origin of *wissenschaft* as a model for seminaries is Friedrich Schleiermacher's (1768–1834) pioneering work at Humboldt University in Berlin. This was rooted in the debate that originated in seventeenth-century England and Holland, of the need for modern theology to be a critical discourse where the parameters are not necessarily set by tradition or Christian doctrine. There was also the need for theology to develop as an academic discipline so that it could be classified as a system of knowledge institutionalized within a university. The goal was no longer the moral and personal formation of individuals through the study of authoritative texts, but in training students in rigorous enquiry in order to move from theory to practical applications.

Schleiermacher's task was to design a curriculum that would train professional ministers for the State Church in Germany, within the context of defending theology's status as an academic discipline. He built on the fourfold structure of traditional theological curriculum from during the Reformation that was used to train pastors and teachers. This consisted of Biblical Studies, Church History, Dogmatics (referred to as Systematic Theology in more recent curriculums), and Practical Theology. He adapted it to a modern university context. While philosophy and history from the four areas of study fit well within the university disciplines, the challenge was to

---

29. Brian Edgar, "The Theology of Theological Education," *Evangelical Review of Theology* 29, no. 3 (2005): 210.

establish practical theology as an academic discipline. For the critics, practical theology was like any other vocational skill, trade or craft that could be taught in a "trade" school such as a seminary and should not be part of a science university. Schleiermacher's argument was that the university had a mandate to train clergymen; their training was no different than that of practitioners of medicine and law. In all three disciplines there was a progression from theory to professional practice.[30] Adopting this model of study was at the loss of *paideia* and personal, moral and spiritual formation.

Schleiermacher's model is still very much the framework that is used in most theological training today, though the specific content of the four areas of study may have changed. There is an understanding that both knowledge and skills are needed for pastoral ministry. Unfortunately, there are few connections between the study of the Bible and theology, and practical ministerial practice. Charles Wood at Southern Methodist University, points out that ministerial practice does not inform the theological disciplines, and there is little relevance between the "important" and "foundational" studies in theology and ministerial practice.[31] However, evangelical seminaries incorporate elements of both the classical and vocational models in their curriculum. There is an emphasis on character formation and the molding of worldview, as well as the "professional studies" required to be a pastor or in some kind of Christian ministry, though the emphasis is on the theory and knowledge.

The last commonly accepted model, **the missional model**, as developed by Robert Banks is referred to as "Jerusalem." The missional model sees mission encompassing all aspects of life – family, friendships, work and neighborhood. For Banks, mission is not just being mission-oriented but "an education undertaken with a view to what God is doing in the world, considered from a global perspective."[32] Therefore theological education is seen as part of mission. It's a model that provides a connection between action and reflection. A missional model of theological education "places the main emphasis on theological mission, on hands-on *partnership* in ministry, based on interpreting the tradition and reflecting on practice with strong spiritual

---

30. Friedrich Schleiermacher and Terrence Tice, *Brief Outline of Theology as a Field of Study: Revised Translation of the 1811 and 1830 Editions,* 3rd ed. (Louisville: Westminster John Knox Press, 2011), 137.
31. Charles Wood, *Vision and Discernment: An Orientation in Theological Studies* (Atlanta: Scholars Press, 1985), 13.
32. Banks, *Reenvisioning Theological Education,* 142.

and communal dimensions."[33] For Banks, the best theological education and spiritual formation is partly field-based, stretching students to do what they are studying, encompassing all of life, and addressing mission opportunities. Classrooms then are in effect "in-service equipping" to be faithful and effective in ministries the students are already involved in. Leadership formation and theological education is most effective when theory and practice, and action and reflection are combined.

The thinking on the three categories has been further developed to incorporate other models of theological education. Brian Edgar, professor at Asbury Theological Seminary, adds a fourth model called **the confessional model**. Referred to as "Geneva," the goal of theological education is to know God through the means of grace and the traditions in a particular faith community, and more specifically through the creed and confession of that community. This involves "formation . . . through *in-formation* about the tradition and *en-culturation* with it."[34] This is done through teaching about the founders, the heroes, the struggles, the strengths, and the traditions that are both distinctive and formative for that community. Examples of this are denominational affiliated seminaries and training institutions of specific mission agencies.

Fig. 1.1 Four Models of Theological Education[35]

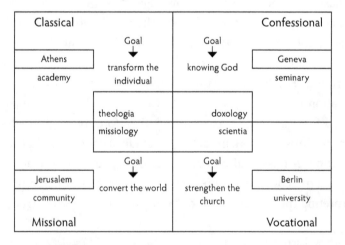

---

33. Ibid., 144.
34. Edgar, *The Theology*, 213.
35. Adapted from Brian Edgar, "The Theology of Theological Education," *Evangelical Review of Theology* 29, no. 3 (2005): 213.

Fig. 1.2 Six Models of Theological Education and Missional Spirituality[36]

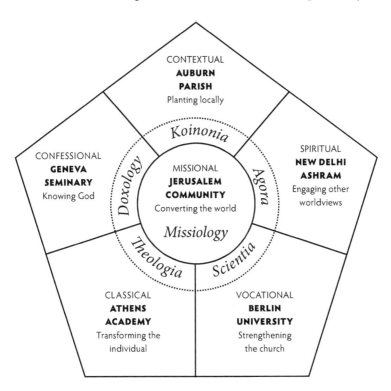

Darren Cronshaw, mission researcher at the Baptist Union of Victoria in Australia, adds two further models.[37] The first is **the contextual model** and referred to as "Auburn." According to Cronshaw, theology and mission need to be expressed in specific contexts such as those in his local neighborhood of Auburn.[38] Bishop Lesslie Newbigin, writing about pastoral ministry states, "I do not think that the geographical parish can ever become irrelevant or marginal. There is a sense in which the primary sense of neighborhood must remain primary, because it is here that men and women relate to each other

36. Adapted from Darren Cronshaw, "Reenvisioning Theological Education and Missional Spirituality," *Journal of Adult Theological Education* 9, no. 1 (2012): 13.
37. Darren Cronshaw, "Reenvisioning Theological Education and Missional Spirituality," *Journal of Adult Theological Education* 9, no. 1 (2012): 9–27.
38. John Franke, *The Character of Theology: An Introduction to Its Nature, Task, and Purpose* (Grand Rapids: Baker Academic, 2005), 90.

simply as human beings and not in respect of their functions in society."[39] So theological training for the contextual model deals with understanding local context and learning how to build community (*koinonia*). The concept is that the "parish" is an "open set" (using terminology from Paul Heibert). The church as a covenant community is a bounded set at the center of the parish (so in effect the parish is a centered set). It is this community that lives out the gospel and in the process the boundaries dissolve. Together they experience community and demonstrate the love of God so that others may belong and one day believe.[40]

The second model that Cronshaw adds is **the spiritual model**, also known as "New Delhi." This is a model for a multicultural and pluralistic world. Cronshaw writes:

> A New Delhi context for missional spirituality is the ashram.[41] As the balance of global power and Christian influence is shifting to the global South, Kraig Klaudt artfully suggests that certain Indian ashrams feature helpful characteristics that theological education can adopt. These ashrams: are located "in the world" without fences; are open to all; offer community living that is engaged in service; emphasize simple living and spiritual maturity more than publishing; provide a holistic curriculum of intellectual, spiritual, political, aesthetic and relational development; and create time and space for spirituality and self-awareness. Locating theological education and missional spirituality in New Delhi reminds me to engage with the worldviews of my neighbors and to welcome the alternative model of the ashram.[42]

---

39. Lesslie Newbigin, *Sign of the Kingdom* (Grand Rapids: Eerdmans, 1981), 64.
40. Stuart Murray, *Church After Christendom* (Bletchley: Paternoster, 2005).
41. An ashram is a hermitage or a monastery. A Christian ashram is a unique place of retreat that is Christ-centered, and where an individual has the opportunity to explore questions regarding the Christian faith and life.
42. Cronshaw, "Reenvisioning Theological Education," 12.

Table 1.1 Models of Theological Education[43]

Symbol	Athens	Berlin	Geneva	Jerusalem	Auburn	New Delhi
Model	Classical	Vocational	Confessional	Missional	Contextual	Spiritual
Context	Academy	University	Seminary	Community	Parish	Ashram
Goal/ Purpose	Transforming the individual	Strengthening the church	Knowing God	Converting the world	Planting locally	Engaging other worldviews
Emphasis	Personal formation: Knowing who . . .	Interpretive skills: Knowing how . . .	In-formation, en-culturation: Knowing what . . .	Mission, partnership: Knowing for . . .	Local, community: Knowing where . . .	Multi-cultural, pluralistic: Knowing others . . .
Formation	Individualized and focused on inner, personal, moral and religious transformation	Clarify vocational identity as the basis for Christian practice	Discursive analysis, comparison and synthesis of beliefs	Learning has to have reference to all dimensions of life, family, friendships, work and neighborhood	Learning how to be relevant locally	Learning to co-exist respectfully while retaining one's identity
Theology	Theology is the knowledge of God, not about God	Theology is a way of thinking, applying theory to life. Theology is applied: spiritual, missio-logical, vocational	Theology is knowing God through a specific tradition	Missiology is the mother of theology. It involves action – mission.	Theology is about being spiritually relevant locally	Theology is about under-standing the revelation of God in other religions and worldviews

---

43. Adapted from Brian Edgar, "The Theology of Theological Education," *Evangelical Review of Theology* 29, no. 3 (2005).

Teacher	Provider: of indirect assistance through intellectual and moral disciplines to help students undergo formation	Professor: The teacher is a researcher whom the students assist	Priest: Knowledge of tradition; lives and exemplifies it as well as knows it	Practioner / missionary: The teacher is not removed from practice; teaching involves sharing lives as well as truth	Pastor: The teacher leads by being relevant in the community	Apologist: Where the teacher not only defends the faith but also builds bridges
Student	Cultivates his mind, character and spirit	Becomes a theoretician able to apply to practice	Initiated into the tradition, beliefs, vocation and ministry	Discipled to become a disciple-maker	Learns to serve the community	Learn to build bridges and defend the faith

5. Theological Training and Need

In order to understand the implications of the six typologies of theological education in today's world, Brian Edgar suggests asking the question, "What is it that makes something *theological* education?"[44] There are six dimensions to the answers:

- *The Content* – that it is about theology and about God.
- *The Purpose* – this would include not only knowledge but also the development of character, holiness and skills for life.
- *The Method* – defines how the training is to be done.
- *The Ethos* – is the individual and communal spirituality that permeates the whole process of education and training.
- *The Context* – identifies where the training takes place.
- *The People* – how does the faith of those involved define the education – both the content and the process?

In looking at the various models of theological training outlined above and connecting them to the context of the church today and the needs of

---

44. Edgar, *The Theology*, 208–217.

the congregations and for appropriate leadership, there are four kinds of theological training.

The first is **training in theology** for the laity in the churches. The purpose is to teach Christians about their faith, to answers their questions and doubts, for them to understand how to express their faith in their churches and community, and to have the appropriate tools to study the Bible. The objective of lay theological training is to enable Christians to find the foundations of and coherence in one's faith.[45]

The second is **training in ministerial theology** for full-time and bi-vocational Christians to become pastors, ministers and teachers for the ministries of the church. The purpose is to equip them to minister effectively through preaching, teaching, discipling, and meet the practical, emotional and social needs of a congregation. In order to do this they need both academic and practical theology. This would include skills in Bible study and biblical exegesis tools, an understanding of the biblical narrative(s) and subsequent church history, systematic and historical theology, as well as a biblical perspective on issues that Christians and the church face today. The practical theology skills would include training in homiletics, teaching, counseling, evangelism, discipling and mentoring. The purpose of any pastoral ministry is defined in Ephesians 4:12–13 "to equip his people for works of service, so that the body of Christ may be built up until we all reach unity in the faith and in the knowledge of the Son of God and become mature, attaining to the whole measure of the fullness of Christ."

The third type is **training in professional theology** for the educators of those involved in ministry. Professional theologians are academics and are not necessarily involved in church ministries but should understand the needs of the church and the various ministries where the graduates minister. They are not only professional theologians but also know how to train ministers of the gospel.

The final type is **training in academic theology**. Situated in a university, academic theology is not necessarily rooted in Christian doctrine, theology or philosophy. It is the study of God and is rooted in anthropology, philosophy and world religions. Schleiermacher is attributed to have been the originator

---

45. Stanley Grenz and Roger Olson, *Who needs Theology? An Invitation to the Study of God* (Downers Grove: InterVarsity Press, 1996), 29–30.

of academic theology. James McClendon, writing about the impact of Schleiermacher on the study of and training in theology, writes:

> In the eyes of his critics, Schleiermacher's liberal Protestantism has reduced theology, understood as doctrines about God, to anthropology, merely doctrines about human states and feelings. But to his followers, he had diminished pretentious rationalism in religion to make room for (affective) faith.
>
> Schleiermacher went on to specify that all Christian proposition can be regarded as descriptions either of human states or of divine attributes, or of the constitution of the world (a triad he made basic to the structure of the *Glaubenslehre*), and pointed out that traditionally all three forms of doctrinal expressions have coexisted.[46]

From the nature of academic theology it is assumed that there is no connection with the local church.

6. Exercises

A. Look at the six models of theological training described in section 4. Identify the strengths and weaknesses of each.

B. What elements of each model would be appropriate for your seminary or Bible college and the context within which it is located?

C. Look at the chart opposite on the four kinds of theological training described in section 5. Identify the type of theological training that your institution is involved in or would like to be involved in. Is there is a different type of theological training that is appropriate for your context? Once you have identified the type of training, fill in the appropriate boxes by answering the questions in each line in detail.

This process will start to define the theological education you provide or would like to provide.

---

46. James Wm. McClendon, Jr., *Systematic Theology: Doctrine, Vol. 2* (Nashville: Abingdon Press, 1994), 26.

	Questions	Theological Training for Laity	Training for Ministerial Theology	Training for Professional Theology	Training for Academic Theology
Content	**What** is the content of the training?				
Purpose	**Why** is this training being done?				
Method	**How** is this training to be done?				
Ethos	What **values** and **spirituality** permeate the training?				
Context	**Where** is the training conducted?				
People	**Who.** How does the **faith of those involved** define the education?				

2

Understanding Effectiveness

1. Organizational Theory

The faculty and the curriculum are not the only determiners for the effectiveness and quality of theological education. Theological training is in the context of an institution, and the effectiveness of the faculty and the curriculum is dependent on the management and administrative support structures that an institution provides. Taken together, they are able to produce the kind of impact desired.

But what is meant by effectiveness? The Organization for Economic Cooperation and Development (OECD) uses a set of criteria to evaluate projects and initiatives. One of the criteria is *effectiveness*. It is it defined as follows:

> [Effectiveness is] a measure of the extent to which an . . . activity attains its objectives. In evaluating the effectiveness of a program or a project, it is useful to consider the following questions:
>
> - To what extent were the objectives achieved / are likely to be achieved?
> - What were the major factors influencing the achievement or non-achievement of the objectives?

To put it very simply – *the effectiveness of an institution is determined by whether it did what it said it was going to do, and got the results that were planned for.* So the institution has to be clear in what it intends to do and has to have the administrative mechanism to determine what the results are.

There needs to be both qualitative and quantitative measures to be able to determine that.

There are two aspects to effectiveness. One is _management effectiveness_ and the other is _programmatic effectiveness_. Each is very different and has different criteria to determine effectiveness. Both together will determine the impact of the institution. Management effectiveness deals with whether the activities that were planned were carried out, whether there was accountability for the funds and resources that the institution has, and whether there is sustainability of the institution. Programmatic effectiveness deals with the impact of the programs (and is addressed in the next chapter) – the results of the activities that were carried out.

In order to have management effectiveness, the institution must have the organizational capacity to accomplish its vision and goals. Organizational theory identifies the different components of any institution, which when taken together determine the capacity of the institution. These are:

- _Vision and Aspiration_ – This defines who the institution is (identity) and why it exists (purpose). It articulates what the institution aspires to do and what it hopes to accomplish. Vision and aspirations are the anchors for the institution in all its planning. The vision and aspirations are determined by the founder(s) and the board, and implemented by the management of the institution.

- _Organizational Structure_ – Every institution has to have a structure in order to operate and have accountability for all its operations, activities and programs. While there are basic principles to structure an institution for effective operations and ensuring accountability, organizational structure is also dependent on cultural values, the personnel available, and the context within which the institution is operating.

- _Human Resources and Personnel_ – Any institution requires people. They need to be recruited, oriented, trained (if necessary), remunerated, managed, and ultimately separated from the institution (through retirement, voluntary departure or termination).

- _Organizational Skills_ – What are the full complement of skills that the institution needs in order to accomplish its mandate and plans? These would include management and administrative skills, as well as technical and/or academic skills needed for its programs.

- *Systems and Infrastructure* – What buildings, facilities, assets (equipment), and infrastructure, as well as systems, does the institution need to operate effectively?
- *Programming* – What is the program(s) that the institution offers in order to accomplish its mandate and plans?
- *External Relations and Networks* – Institutions do not exist in isolation. In order to be effective, they need to maintain relationships with external organizations, other institutions and government departments, as well as being part of networks of institutions that are involved in similar programming.
- *Organizational Culture* – Every institution has a culture that is based on the values of the institution as a whole, as well as those of the founder(s), leadership, employees, faculty and students. There needs to be intentionality in the kind of culture that is desired, in order to facilitate the effectiveness of the institution.
- *Sustainability* – An institution does not just exist in the present only, but needs to ensure its sustainability in the long term. The factors that ensure sustainability are funding, personnel, assets and resources.
- *Financial Management* – All institutions need to have systems to not only account for the funds it receives and the assets it possesses, but also be able to manage them effectively and report on them to senior management and to donors.

So the starting point to determining an institution's effectiveness is to assess whether the institution has the necessary organizational capacity.

2. Organizational Capacity Assessment

So how is organizational capacity assessed?

An organizational capacity assessment is NOT an audit or a compliance assessment tool that is administered. There is no judgment or grading at the end of the process. A capacity assessment is both a process of learning lessons from the past and building the capacity of the institution so that it can improve its effectiveness. The main purpose of such a process is to identify areas of organizational strengths and weaknesses. It is meant to provide a detailed profile of the organization for the board, the management and other stakeholders to understand it better. The final objective of the assessment is to determine how the organization can become more effective in fulfilling its God given mandate and vision.

Assessment Process

Before starting the assessment process it is important to determine the scope of the organizational assessment. Is it an assessment of the management and administrative capacities only, or should the programs also be assessed? There are questions as well about the legal structure of the organization within the country that need to be answered:

- What is the institution registered as in the country? Is there a specific category it is registered under?
- Is the institution part of national or international networks or associations? Is it part of a denomination?

The organizational assessment needs to be done in a participatory manner. In order to ensure this, the assessment team should consist of representatives from management, administration and faculty, as well as at least one board member. In some cases (where appropriate) a student representative may also be included.

a) In preparation for the assessment, the senior leadership of the institution needs to brief all the relevant stakeholders and leadership within the institution about both the purpose and method of the organizational assessment.

b) The assessment team should consist of a team leader, and representatives of management, administration, faculty, board and students (if appropriate). It is critical that the participatory nature of the assessment be maintained at all times.

c) Before the assessment starts, the team leader needs to obtain assurance from the board and senior management of the institution for full cooperation of staff during the assessment process. Every effort must be made by the team leader to reduce the sense of threat that an assessment can raise and affirm to the leadership and staff that this is not a judgment but a process to increase effectiveness.

d) Under the leadership of the assessment team leader, the full team should meet for at least half a day to determine how the assessment will be carried out. The following questions and issues need to be addressed:

- Which departments and individuals need to be interviewed?
- What documents and explanation of processes do you expect the departments and staff to have ready before the interview?
- What is the schedule of the interviews?
- How will the team interview the individuals or departments? Will the assessment team be broken into smaller teams or will the whole assessment team interview each department and individual? There may be times when the larger team is broken into smaller teams, while at other times the whole team may choose to be present.
- For each interview, identify who will lead in asking the questions and who will be taking notes.

e) At the end of each day, at least an hour should be set aside to review the day and identify specific issues and trends noticed.

f) At the end of each day, the team leader, along with help from others, should start compiling the final report.

g) At the end of the assessment process, a formal presentation should be made to the appropriate leadership of the institution – the management and board. A written draft copy of the report should be given as well as an oral presentation. This will provide an opportunity for the leadership to understand the issues raised and to seek clarification, and then to provide feedback to the assessment team. Only then should a final report be submitted.

The use of the assessment tool and the assessment process is a capacity building exercise for the institution as a whole, as they begin to understand organizational development focusing on organizational capacity, training needs, development of systems and infrastructure, and the need for technology, equipment and other assets as appropriate. At the end of the assessment, the board and the leadership will mutually agree upon an action plan for organizational capacity development.

3. Exercise

Conduct an organizational capacity assessment of your institution using the toolkit below and the guidelines described above.

The Organizational Capacity Assessment Toolkit

The toolkit looks at all aspects of the organization. These include:

- Vision and aspiration
- Organizational structure
- Human resources and personnel
- Organizational skills
- Systems and infrastructure
- Programming
- External relations and networks
- Organizational culture
- Sustainability
- Financial management

Each category in the toolkit will have a question or a statement which seeks to identify whether a specific system or process exists, a specific task is done, or specific documents exists. Each of this is then rated as follows.

Rating Scale

1 – Not evident or non-existent within the organization (Needs Improvement)

2 – Evident or existing (Good)

3 – Evident or existing and of excellent quality (Very Good)

The 1, 2, and 3 are not grades or marks than can be added up for a score. It merely indicates what exists and the quality of it.

While some items may be very clear to rate based on whether they exist or not, for others a subjective judgment is made by the technical members of the team. You may choose to add comments or observations where appropriate, which would clarify or explain the rating.

Table 2.1. Organizational Capacity Assessment Tool[1]

Functional Area	Criteria	Rating			Comments
		3	2	1	
		Very Good	Good	Needs Improve-ment	
Mission Vision and Values	The institution is able to operationalize the vision or mission				
	The institution's vision or mission is understood by all staff				
Theological Position	The institution has a clearly articulated and biblical theological position				
	The institution has a clearly articulated doctrinal position				
	The institution is able to function in a pluralistic context				
Integral Mission	The institution is able to integrate the spiritual and social dimension of Christian witness at a program and community level				

---

1. Adapted from the Canadian Baptist Ministries' (CBM) *Organizational Capacity Assessment Toolkit* developed by Rupen Das and modified for seminaries by Colin Godwin.

Functional Area	Criteria	Rating			Comments
		3	2	1	
		Very Good	Good	Needs Improve-ment	
Theological Education and Leadership Formation	The institution is part of a denomination or has denominational partners who value the institution's goal to train its leaders in theology and practice of ministry				
	There are qualified trainers and educators available				
	The theological training programs are accredited by national, regional or international bodies				
	The training institutions are accountable to the denominational leadership (where appropriate)				
	Graduate level programs in theological education are available in the primary language of learning				
	Recently trained graduates are assimilated into the life and witness of the denomination, as pastors, evangelists and church-workers				

Functional Area	Criteria	Rating			Comments
		3 Very Good	**2** Good	**1** Needs Improve-ment	
Curriculum and Professors	The institution reviews its curriculum every five years in order to adapt the courses taught in the institution to the challenges faced by graduates and by the church today.				
	The institution recruits teachers who have training in educational theory and practice.				
	The institution recruits professors who have the appropriate ministry and academic qualifications				
	Recent graduates are suitably equipped to continue their education in other institutions (i.e. masters or doctoral degrees)				
	The current curriculum equips church leaders in all areas of ministry				
Institutional Structure	The institution has a clearly defined institutional structure with roles and responsibilities				
	Job descriptions exist for all paid positions				
	The management of the institution has a board or committee providing oversight				
	The board or committee has a broad range of skills, is gender sensitive and has appropriate appointment procedures				
	The board or committee understands its role and functions effectively				

Functional Area	Criteria	Rating			Comments
		3	2	1	
		Very Good	Good	Needs Improvement	
Human Resources and Personnel	Positions within the institution are clearly identified				
	There are clear job descriptions for each identified position				
	Most positions are filled by people with the appropriate skills, training and experience, and with no gender, tribal or "personal connection" bias				
	The institution is able to recruit the kind of people that it needs				
	There are clear personnel policies that guide every aspect of the human resource function				
	The institution's salary structure is fair and is competitive in attracting and retaining good quality staff.				
	The policies concerning hiring and dismissal are clearly stated and are regulated by appropriate school personnel				

Functional Area	Criteria	Rating			Comments
		3 **Very Good**	**2** **Good**	**1** **Needs Improve-ment**	
Institutional Skills	The institution is able to measure and manage its own performance and make adjustments accordingly				
	The institution is able to monitor its operating environment and landscape, and understand the implications of changes for the institution				
	The institution is able to do strategic and operational planning				
	The institution is able to do financial planning and budgeting				
	The institution is able to do human resource planning				
	The institution is able to fund raise and generate revenue				
Church Planting and Witness	The institution is involved in denominational plans for church planting and witness				
	Students are trained in evangelism and church planting				
	Continuing training is offered to pastors and church leaders				

Functional Area	Criteria	Rating			Comments
		3 Very Good	**2** Good	**1** Needs Improve-ment	
Systems and Infrastructure	Planning is done regularly				
	There are fairly clear processes and frameworks for decision making				
	The institution has adequate physical infrastructure in terms of buildings, office space, etc.				
	The institution has vehicles and other appropriate transportation to visit projects, churches, etc.				
	The institution has the appropriate technology in adequate numbers to be effective				
	There is a library that is organized with adequate staff and equipment, including computers, with an adequate budget and plans for growth				

Functional Area	Criteria	Rating			Comments
		3	**2**	**1**	
		Very Good	Good	Needs Improve-ment	
External Relations and Accreditation	Part of Networks: The institution is a part of a network that: Increases educational value and prevents duplication of efforts				
	Helps the institution gain greater recognition and credibility among governments and international donors and faith-based organizations				
	Strengthens the institution's own capacity to develop and implement good programs				
	Access to Other Funding & Donors: The institution has established relationships with other funders and donors nationally and internationally				
	Accreditation: The institution issues degrees as an institution accredited by the appropriate national authority				
Institutional Culture	There is a culture of excellence and performance is routinely acknowledged				
	The institutional culture encourages people to stay within the institution				

Functional Area	Criteria	Rating			Comments
		3	2	1	
		Very Good	Good	Needs Improve-ment	
Sustainability	The institution has a viable sustainability strategy which can: Diversify and increase the number of different income sources				
	Reduce financial dependency on funds received from any one source				
	The institution shows potential for expansion because: The institution has shown a steady rate of growth over the last five years				
	Programs and human resource development initiatives to date have improved management and technical capabilities within the institution				
	The institution has the management and technical resources necessary to increase programming				

Functional Area	Criteria	Rating			Comments
		3	2	1	
		Very Good	Good	Needs Improve-ment	
Finance	A qualified finance and accounting professional provides oversight to the administration functions of the institution				
	An annual financial audit is conducted by a qualified independent auditor				
	Adequate computers systems are available for administration				
	Professional accounting software is utilized in the administration of the institution				
	Banking relationships are established and robust				
	A hierarchical management structure is in place within finance administration and accountability				
	There exists a system for management reporting and reporting of financial results to leadership				
	An independent appointed Board of Directors provides oversight to management				
	Budgeting and financial controls are internal activities and have adequate reporting procedures in place				

Once the assessment is done, review the chart above and use the Summary and Recommendations chart below to summarize the following:

- Strengths of the institution
- Areas for improvement and recommendations of how they could be done

- Areas of concern and strategies to mitigate the problem or vulnerability
- Any additional summary comments

Table 2.2. Summary and Recommendations

Strengths of the Institution	
Areas for Improvement by the Institution	
	Recommendations
Areas of Concern for the Institution and Strategies for Mitigation	
Summary Comments	

3

Connecting Curriculum with Context

Program effectiveness is not only internally focused on the quality of the program but identifies results and assesses if the results were accomplished. The results are not how many graduated, but what the graduates accomplished in their places of ministry – the ministry for which they were prepared. "Results" is a very threatening term because it implies success or failure.[1] "Results" also implies a very high degree of accountability – that the resources available were used properly to achieve stated goals and objectives. The challenge with using "results" language in education beyond the classroom is that there are too many uncontrollable factors that influence what a graduate is able to achieve in their ministry context after leaving the seminary.

While all this may be true, there has to be an *intentional connection* between the context(s) where graduates will minister and the curriculum used to train the students. If the connection is well understood and properly thought through, and the resulting curriculum is relevant to the context, there is a high probability that the graduates will on the whole be effective in their places of ministry. This intentional connection does not just look at the needs in the context for which the graduates need to be prepared for, but the graduates need to understand the values of the society, the ways they

---

1. The understanding of results in ministry is not necessarily the numbers of people who were converted, or joined the church or are in Bible studies. While these are reasonable indicators of results, conversions are something that God the Holy Spirit brings about. The understanding of results in this book is what changed in a ministry context or in individuals as a result of what the graduate did. This may include conversions, but that is not the sole indicator.

perceive and understand God and spiritual matters, what they dream and aspire to, and the way they process information and how they learn. Each of these needs to influence, not only how the courses are taught, but also the content of the courses. The theology they are taught needs to be relevant in the contexts where they will minister.

But how does one connect curriculum with context so that the graduates are effective?

1. Understanding the Connection of Curriculum to Context

The field of community development, which over the past many decades has been under severe criticism and pressure to show results for the huge amounts of funds that it receives, may offer some insights on how to connect curriculum with context. In order to respond to this criticism, development professionals have had to create a structured discipline in analyzing problems and designing appropriate responses to ensure that the specific problems were addressed. It was not enough to show that activities were carried out, but projects had to show that change had taken place. Some lessons that may be relevant:

A. An intervention, project, program or service delivery needs to be based on a needs assessment and a problem analysis. This will identify specific issues and/or problems that need to be addressed and thus moves decisions away from a subjective feeling of what one thinks should be done. The focus is on being relevant and on responding to needs.

B. Developing the logic of a program is critical to its relevance and effectiveness (success). The focus is on the "outcome" level – which is the main context that needs to be addressed. Any training that is done has to address the needs at the outcome level. What this means is that a particular action will result in a change. In development theory, this is visualized as follows:

Figure 3.1. A Logic Model of a Program

A Logic Chain

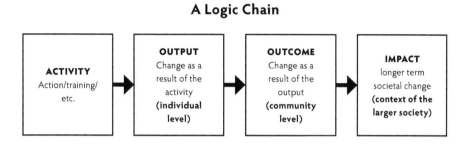

In trying to understand this model of connecting curriculum with context, there are a number of key points to keep in mind.

- An activity like training is for a purpose and not an end in itself. So comments like, how many people were trained, have little relevance, unless what they did with their training is assessed. An activity is only the first step in a process that will produce results.

- An activity or training has to produce change. A completed activity is not an "output." A completed activity only indicates that the training took place. It does not indicate if any learning took place or not. It cannot be assumed that learning took place.

There are two levels at which the effectiveness of the training is assessed.

i. *Did learning take place?* This is evaluated through tests, exams, case studies, assignments, projects and so on. An output assesses what changed as a result of the training – what changed in the student's understanding of an issue; what changed in their skill level; what changed in terms of them gaining additional knowledge; what changed in terms of their attitude? Usually the changes are assessed at the knowledge, skills or behavior, and attitude levels. A "graduate profile" has relevance at the output level as it identifies the changes that need to be accomplished as a result of the training by the time a student graduates. In the discipline of education, these are referred to as educational outcomes – what has been learned as a result of the education or training.

ii.   The second level of effectiveness of the training is to determine and evaluate *whether what was learned was actually used.* This is critical, since learning is not an end in itself but is for a purpose. This use of the learning and the resulting impact is referred to as an "outcome" (different than an educational outcome).

- The effectiveness of an activity or training is actually assessed at the outcome level. Did the graduate use what they learned, and how effective was it in addressing issues in their context of ministry or in communicating spiritual truth? The training is conducted so that there would be changes or effectiveness at the outcome (community/church) level.

- The training actually can also influence society, not just the community, the church, or any other context of ministry. However, any activity only contributes to longer-term societal change along with other factors and influences. It is rarely the sole cause of the changes in society.

The example that follows highlights the difference between an **activity**, a **completed activity**, an **output** and an **outcome**. A non-theological, very simple example is being used to highlight these differences.

An Example of Program Logic

Highlighting the Difference between an Activity, a Completed Activity, and Output and an Outcome

Based on an assessment in the community, it was found out that there was a very high degree of malnutrition among the children. Upon closer analysis, it was found that the cause of the malnutrition was due to the fact that the mothers did not cook balanced nutritious meals.

So a training program was designed and organized to teach the mothers to cook nutritious meals. The <u>assumption</u> was that if the mothers knew how to cook nutritious meals, then they would do so, and the number of cases of malnutrition among the children would decrease.

The training that was conducted was the **activity**.

When the training was completed, it is then called a **completed activity**.

A completed activity only implies that the training took place. There is no understanding if anything was learned. What is not known is whether the mothers saw this time during the training as a time away from their husbands and children, not having any household responsibilities, and a time of good fellowship with other women? Or did the mothers see the training as a time to learn about nutritious meals and help their children? So when the mothers are asked for their comments and feedback as part of the evaluation of the training, and they say, "It was really good and helpful; we should have more times like this" – what do they actually mean? As important as the participant feedback and evaluation of the training is, just as important is the need to assess what was learned, what changes took place in the mothers' understanding of diet and healthy meals, and most importantly, how did their behavior change – were they able to actually cook the healthy meals.

This change in their understanding of diet and nutrition, and any changes in their behavior and actions as a result of the training, is called an **output**. An output and a completed activity are not the same.

A completed activity and an output have still not caused any changes in the health of their children. Just because they know about nutritious meals and are able to cook such meals, does not mean that they actually went back home and cooked the meals. The only evidence that the training was successful and effective is if the level of malnutrition of the children decreases. That was the objective of the training.

The decrease in the level of malnutrition in the children as a result of the mothers cooking healthy meals is called an **outcome**. The training is directly connected to the problems and issues in the context.

Summarizing

An understanding of context (a needs assessment, a context analysis) was key in designing the training program. Conducting the training program was the **activity**. Once the training program was successfully run, it is then a **completed activity**. Assessing what changed in the understanding, attitudes and behavior of the participants is called the **output**. Once the learning from the training is used in the context and changes take place there, that is referred to as an **outcome**.

This type of program logic, where an action or activity has a result, has a number of implications for theological education.

i.   Most theological education programs focus on the truths that need to be learned. Focusing on context (outcome level) means that it is not just the content of the truth that needs to be understood, but that the student needs to understand how to communicate the truth in a way that the people in the place of ministry will understand it. What cultural and philosophical factors will influence how people understand the truth? How do people hear and understand any type of communication, since people process information differently and have different learning styles?

ii. The implications of this are that the responsibility of training institutions does not end at the output level (at the time of graduation), ensuring that students meet the requirements of the "graduate profile." If the training is to be effective and relevant, then it must have an effect at the outcome level – on the church or place of ministry. If there are no significant changes at the outcome level (in the community or church where the graduate is ministering), then either the training was ineffective or was not relevant. This then becomes one of the bases (but not the only one) on which a program is evaluated. The responsibility of the seminary does not end with the student graduating, but in ensuring that the graduate is effective in their place of ministry. Only then can the seminary be sure that the education and training provided was effective.

iii. An assessment of needs, problems and dynamics at the outcome (community/church) and impact (society) levels determines the type of activity or training that is conducted. In the contexts where the graduates will be ministering, what are issues and problems that people are dealing with; what are their understandings of Scriptural truths; how open or resistant are they to the gospel? The purpose of the training is to bring about change at the outcome (community/church) level and contribute to change at the impact (society) level.

iv. There is a need to regularly monitor the changes in the context(s) at the outcome (community/church) and impact (society) levels to ensure that the training remains relevant.

v. There needs to be administrative mechanisms that provide information and feedback from changes at the output, outcome and impact levels to the leadership of the seminary so that proper decisions about curriculum redesign or course revisions can be made.

2. Designing a Feedback Mechanism

In being able to connect curriculum with context, there are two factors that are critical in order to ensure effectiveness. The first factor is that there needs to be administrative mechanisms that ensure feedback is collected. The second factor is that there needs to be clear administrative mechanisms for decisions to be made based on the feedback and information that has been gathered.

A. *Feedback Mechanism* – An education institution needs to have a feedback mechanism to assess progress of the programs, as well as to ensure that the institution is being well run. An exam, for example, assesses the progress of the student. A monthly financial report provides a snapshot in time of the financial status of the organization. In the same way there needs to be mechanisms at the activity, output and outcome levels that gather information and provide feedback on progress and changes taking place.

B. *Decision Making* – Good decisions are made on the basis of accurate information and feedback from various parts of the organization. It is not uncommon that a program evaluation is done and then simply filed away, without looking at the findings and determining what needs to change. All the feedback and information gathered needs to be clearly channeled to appropriate decision-makers so that the information can be assessed and the right decisions made.

A feedback mechanism for a seminary could look like the following.

Figure 3.2. Organizational Assessments and Model for Feedback

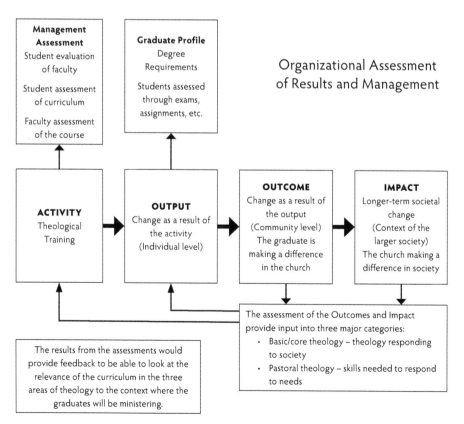

A number of key points from Figure 3.2:

- Before a curriculum is designed or revised, a detailed assessment has to be done of the various contexts where the graduates of the program will be ministering, whether they are churches or communities, as well as the social, religious and political contexts of the communities. This assessment will be critical in determining the content of the curriculum.

- As each activity/course is conducted and then completed, the effectiveness of the activity needs to be assessed (management assessments). While the assessment by the faculty of how they felt the course went is very important, the feedback from the students on the course is equally important on whether they thought the course was relevant, and whether they thought the faculty taught the material in a way that was clear and easily understood, as well as making it relevant to their ministry context. This feedback needs to go to the Academic Dean, who then works with the concerned faculty in making the necessary adjustment to that specific course, if required.

- The seminary's main function is to equip leaders. The output, then, is that leaders are properly and adequately equipped. This is the easiest level of assessment. Most seminaries have already established "graduate profiles" or "graduation requirements" for every program that it runs. Throughout their tenure at a seminary, students are continually being assessed as to whether they are in the process of fulfilling the graduation requirements. This is done through tests, exams, assignments, projects, case studies and so on. The *changes* in the student's knowledge, attitudes and behavior/ skills are what is being assessed.

While the graduate profile or graduation requirement (outputs) focus on the students' performance, their performance also provides a wealth of information about specific courses. Were there specific courses that most of the students found extremely easy or very difficult? After understanding the cause(s) of the students' performance, these courses may need to be redesigned.

Any seminary's mission should never be to only equip leaders. Equipped leaders need to serve. A seminary's mission should be to serve the church and mission agencies involved in the Great Commission and the Great Commandment, and they do that by equipping leaders. Measuring the outcome, therefore, is by assessing whether the church and mission organizations are being served by the graduates. The right tools are needed to answer this question and the assessment needs to be done by working closely with the churches and ministry contexts where the graduates are serving.

At the outcome level, periodic assessments of ministry contexts of the graduates (churches and/or communities) would provide a wealth of information for the redesign of the curriculum or revision of specific courses. Feedback from the graduates, the church community, key Christian leaders, as well as the community, will provide information for the revision of the three aspects of theological education:

A. *Basic/Core Theological Truths* – These would include the Creeds, Systematic or Biblical Theology, and Historical Theology. While all theological concepts are important for any theological education, are specific theological concepts problematic in particular contexts (such as the concept of Jesus being the Son of God in an Islamic context, or Jesus being the only God in a Hindu context). Students need to not only know what these are, but also understand how to address them.

B. *Contextual Theology* – How is God perceived and understood in a particular context or culture? The issue of Christian ethics in various contexts is critical. What are biblical perspectives on the issues of poverty and social justice, gender, race, human trafficking, immigrants, female genital mutilation and so on? What are specific social and ethical issues in a particular context that need to be addressed from within a Christian ethical framework? How is respect shown, and thus God worshiped, in a specific culture and context?

C. *Pastoral Theology* – Are individuals and families struggling with specific issues that a graduate would know how to address? Examples of issues include child raising and child discipline, husband-wife relationships and divorce, issues with in-laws in extended family situations, sexual orientation, selection of marriage partners, etc. Pastoral issues may also encompass problems related with recent converts such as persecution, baptism, being cut off from their family and community, polygamy, and so on.

Feedback from assessments, student and faculty evaluations, and student performance need to be directed to specific educational administrators who have the ability to make the decisions regarding redesign of the curriculum or revision of specific courses. Too often evaluations are done, but the information is never used to make the educational program more relevant.

3. Frequency and Methods of Assessments

Assessments and feedback mechanisms can be overwhelming to manage if they are not properly scheduled. The data gathered needs to be organized in ways so that the right decisions are made. The following chart identifies the various assessments and feedbacks, who participates in them, how often are they conducted and the method of collecting the data.

Table 3.1. Frequency and Methods of Assessments

ACTIVITY			
Content	**Participants**	**Methodology**	**Frequency**
1. Feedback on a course by student and faculty	Faculty and students	Course evaluation	At the end of every course
OUTPUT			
Content		**Methodology**	**Frequency**
1. Output from the educational program	Students	Fulfill graduation requirements by passing exams, completing assignments, projects, etc.	Once a year
2. Graduate profile	Students	Self-assessment	

OUTCOME			
Content		Methodology	Frequency
Self-Assessment What from the seminary are they using? What from the seminary are they not using? What do they wish they had learned at the seminary? In what ways are they making a difference? Preaching/teaching Discipleship Ministry to families/children/youth Evangelism Addressing social needs – the poor and the marginalized Conflict management Church governance/structure Are there specific issues or challenges that the church or community faces that the pastor needs new skills or insight/teaching?	Graduates	Questionnaire, primarily qualitative with some quantitative This will be followed by a one-on-one interview	Every 2–3 years
The Church Community Assesses the pastor in each of the above areas Assesses its own faith journey	The church where the graduate is ministering	Focus groups	

IMPACT			
Content		**Methodology**	**Frequency**
Perceptions of the church and its effectiveness/ impact/influence by: Key church leaders Outsiders/non-believers	Key church leaders and outsiders in the areas where the graduates are ministering	Key informant interviews	
2. How is the church involved with the community and society in responding to need through service delivery, development projects and/or advocacy? How is the church integrating the good news of the kingdom of God into the demonstration of the reality of the kingdom?	Leaders and members of the community where the graduate's church is ministering	Interviews, visits to the church's programs	Every 5–7 years
3. What is society's understanding of: God (Christ, Trinity, etc.) The Bible The church Salvation Is the seminary preparing student to address these issues as perceived by society?	Key church leaders and possibly theologians	Key informant interviews	
4. What competing messages are out there and what media are they using? Is the seminary teaching its students to find a place in this crowded field and be effective in communicating?	Key church leaders, sociologists and other commentators on social issues	Key informant interviews and research of data that is available from a variety of sources	

It is important to recognize that there has to be an organization-wide commitment to gathering feedback and ensuring the relevant changes are taking place. The process has to be led by the senior management of the institution. However, there has to be a designated person to design and implement the process of assessments and gathering feedback, organizing the data, and ensuring that they get to the right decision-maker. Without a designated person, the process will not happen.

4. Assessing Effectiveness

An assessment process such as this not only connects curriculum with context, but is also a process to assess the effectiveness of the institution and its educational program. Feedback from the graduates, the churches and ministry contexts where the graduates are serving, as well as key Christian leaders, will provide information as to whether the leaders whom the seminary has trained are being effective.

Based on an understanding of the context, the seminary may develop specific indicators at the church and community level to determine if they are accomplishing their goals and vision. These indicators can be *quantitative* in that they measure changes that have taken place or activities that have been initiated. Or they can be *qualitative*, where they describe what a situation looks like, whether it has moved closer to the ideal that had been planned for.

A seminary has to have some way of determining whether it is accomplishing its goals and objectives. *Management indicators* track whether the activities planned have taken place. These would include issues such as how many students graduated, did the seminary stay within the budget that had been planned, is fundraising on track to meet the seminary's goals, are the right students and the right number of students being recruited, does the seminary have the faculty it needs, does the seminary have the facilities and resources to conduct the educational programs. *Program indicators* on the other hand look at the impact of the educational program. These look at issues such as the students' understanding of the Bible, theology and ministry change, how effective were the graduates in their places of ministry, and how communities and society are being influenced by the churches and the ministries that the graduates are involved in.

Management and program indicators taken together provide feedback on the effectiveness of seminaries. Below is an example from the Arab Baptist Theological Seminary (ABTS) in Beirut, Lebanon, on developing indicators at the outcome and impact levels. At the outcome level they developed indicators to assess the seminary as (i) serving the churches, (ii) providing specialized resources, (iii) equipping faithful men and women, (iv) whether the graduates' ministries were perceived as being effective, and finally (v) whether Jesus Christ was being proclaimed as Lord.

Figure 3.3 ABTS Model with Indicators for Assessing Effectiveness

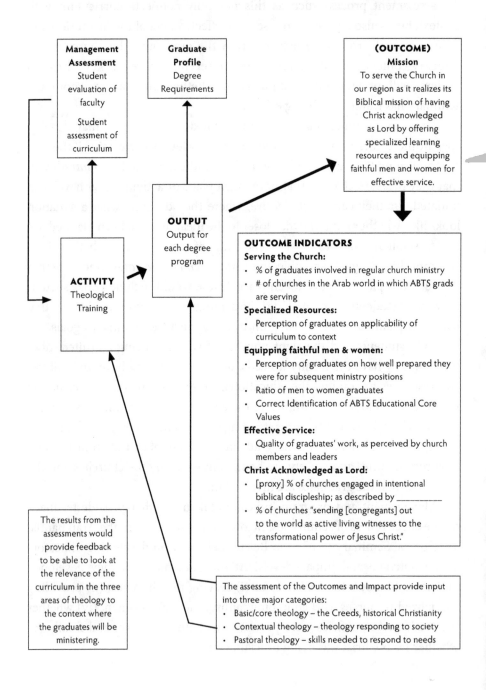

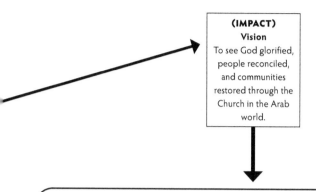

(IMPACT)
Vision
To see God glorified,
people reconciled,
and communities
restored through the
Church in the Arab
world.

TO SEE GOD GLORIFIED:
Churches unified in worship, singing
"**Worthy is the Lord** – and Jesus, the Lamb who was slain - to receive honor, power and praise"
and engaging in worship that **completely transforms**
thoughts and attitudes.
Where people encounter the divine, and are compelled to
go and declare His wonders;
telling stories of God's love and grace.

PEOPLE RECONCILED:
When individuals
and groups experience
the unimaginable extent
of God's forgiveness,
and the **undeserved work**
He did on the cross
to reunite humankind to Himself
inspiring those in conflict to
forgive previous offences
and **extend grace** across
socioeconomic
religious,
ethnic,
tribal, and
political lines.

COMMUNITIES RESTORED:
Where once sin and injustice were the norm
peace, justice, and equality define the
relationships
within neighborhoods, towns, cities…
Physical needs are met as groups
share what they have,
resolve issues of injustice,
and **serve** each other
in sacrificial love
Emotional and relational needs are satisfied as
people cultivate the
deep,
diverse,
and fulfilling relationships
they were designed for.

- Under each, there were *quantitative* indicators such as the percentage of graduates involved in regular church ministry, number of churches in the Arab world where ABTS graduates are serving, ratio of men to women graduates, etc.
- Or there were *qualitative* indicators such as, perception of the graduates as to the applicability of the curriculum to the context, quality of the graduates' work as perceived by church members and leaders, etc.

The interviews, focus groups and survey that are done as part of the assessment of the context to redesign the curriculum or revise courses, will also provide the information to determine the effectiveness of the seminary. It does not have to be a separate process.

Developing indicators and measuring the influence of the seminary at the impact level is extremely difficult. It would almost be impossible to use quantitative indicators. In the example below, ABTS decided to use word pictures to describe the biblical visions of society, namely God glorified, people reconciled, and communities restored. With these being the ideals, the questions that were asked was whether the churches where the graduates ministered understood that this is the kind of transformation that God intended for his creation and that he was looking for partners through whom to work.

5. Exercise - Organizing the Process

The process of connecting curriculum with context starts with a realization of the need for relevance of the seminary and its graduates in the communities where they serve. There are two models of organizations. One model focuses on roles, lines of accountability, and ensuring efficient processes. The focus is internal and the objective is to have a high quality and effectively functioning organization. The other model is based on the understanding that an institution is an organism that functions with a specific environment and context. In order to survive it needs to continually adapt to its environment without losing its integrity, and its vision, mission and mandate. It is continually involved in maintaining a delicate balance between who it is and relevance to the context in which it lives. The two models are not necessarily exclusive of each other, but rather have different emphases.

Once there is an organization-wide commitment to becoming this type of organization, the senior leadership has to identify a team to lead this process. While there needs to be one designated person, they would lead a team that consists of faculty members and administrators. This team would do the following:

- They would identify existing feedback mechanisms that already collected data and information. These could be student evaluations of courses, faculty feedback on courses, and the different ways the progress and performance of the students are assessed (tests, exams, assignments, projects, etc.). A system then needs to be designed to organize this information so that it is useable by the administrators to make decisions about course revisions and curriculum redesign.

- The team would then look at the various contexts where their graduates are ministering. Periodic assessments then need to be organized. These assessments would consist of the following:
  a) Graduate interviews – this could be using focus groups and/or individual interviews
  b) Church interviews (both leadership and the congregation) – this would usually be through focus groups
  c) Community interviews – conduct some interviews in the community where the church is located to assess the community's perception of the church
  d) Key Christian leader interviews – Christian leaders should also be interviewed with regards to the seminary and its graduates
  e) Other individual interviews – interviews with other Christian leaders, theologians, sociologists, and thinkers

At some point, there needs to be a larger assessment on how society is changing and what are the prevailing understandings of God, the basic tenets of the Christian faith, as well what are social and religious trends in society.

Examples of questionnaires and assessment templates are in the **Appendix**. Each institution needs to develop its own questionnaires and determine whom it will interview and the methods to be used for data collection.

- Once the data collection is done, the team then analyzes the information and makes recommendations as to the changes that need to be made.

- This report is then provided to the senior management of the institution to make the appropriate decisions, with the approval of the board of the institution.
- A separate report may also be provided on whether the seminary is being effective, based on indicators that had been developed.

4

Managing Change and Being an Agent of Change

Any change in an institution is threatening to most people. Moving towards becoming an institution that responds to its context in order to be relevant will require changes in its organizational structure, its systems and policies, and in the way it has always functioned. There are very strong emotions involved when people feel threatened by change. These usually are fear, resistance and insecurity. Staff members may feel that they will lose their jobs or their positions of responsibility and influence. Or it may be that some staff members are comfortable in their positions and do not like change. It is important to realize that becoming an institution that is relevant to its context requires change in not only in the content of its curriculum, but that the changes will be multidimensional. There will need to be:

- Changes in aspirations and identity
- Changes in processes and systems
- Changes in curriculum
- Changes in attitudes
- Changes in skills required
- Changes in expectations
- Changes in structure
- Changes in staffing patterns and requirements
- Changes in type of leadership

So the process of change has to be managed properly if it is to avoid disaster.

1. Managing the Process of Change

There are three ways that organizations experience change:

- Leadership impose the change
- External circumstances, such as reduced funding, or change in government legislation, force change
- Change can be brought about through a participatory process to ensure that the ownership for the changes are embraced by everyone within the organization

While there are some cultural patterns of leadership where leaders are expected to make the decisions and impose the necessary changes, the long-term effectiveness of the organization depends on all staff members believing in what the organization does, and therefore actively participating in the process of change.

Change that is sustainable is participatory and is a process. It involves everyone in the organization and key stakeholders of the organization. It is also a process that involves detailed planning and a scheduled progression. Figure 4.1 shows the overall process.

a) The beginning of the process of change starts with a recognition that change is desired, and sometimes, because of circumstances, is required. This may have been recognized by only key leadership or more widely across the institution.

b) While there may be recognition that changes need to take place, an intentional decision by the senior leadership needs to be made.

c) Once the decision is made to move ahead with the changes, the support of the key stakeholders needs to be sought. These may include the board, the organization that represents the staff and faculty, major donors, etc.

d) Once that support is received, a participatory process is used to create a vision for the planned changes, to ensure a commitment of the majority of the staff and faculty, and to ensure that the capacity to institute the changes is available within the organization.

e) At this point, the planning for the changes begins. The first step is to assess and identify what needs to change; for example, what aspects of the curriculum will be impacted, what are the faculty needs, what policies need to change and so on.

Figure 4.1. Process for Organizational Change

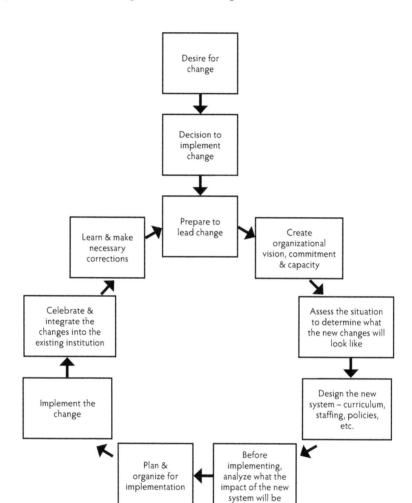

f) The second step in planning is to design the new system – the curriculum, the policies, the organizational structure to support the new system, identifying the skill sets required to make the new system work, etc.

g) Once the design is completed, an analysis needs to be done to determine the impact of the changes. Will this increase or decrease the enrolment of students? Will the new curriculum (for example) be attractive to prospective students? Will churches and mission organizations hire graduates from the revised educational program? Can the institution find the faculty for the courses being offered? Is there adequate funding for the revised curriculum?

h) Now the process for planning to implement is done. The issues that need to be identified are (1) identify all the tasks that need to be done; (2) schedule each of the tasks as to when each one will be done; (3) identify the timeframe as to when each task should be completed; and finally (4) identify who is responsible for ensuring each task is completed exactly as planned.

i) Only when the previous step is planned in detail can the implementation start.

j) Once the implementation is completed, there should be a visible celebration involving everyone, thanking people for their support and involvement, and signifying the inauguration of the new system or curriculum. At this point, the change management team needs to ensure that the new system or curriculum is integrated into the existing systems of the institution.

k) The final step is to identify lessons learned, make the necessary corrections and decide if further changes need to be made.

Following such a process ensures that problems and challenges in any change process are dealt with systematically at various points in the process.

2. Being an Agent of Change

Successful change programs in institutions are led by individuals who are agents of change. It is important to understand how you as a leader perceive and handle change.

Reflect on the following questions:

- Over the past twelve months, what significant changes have I personally made?
- Do I try to anticipate external changes and act on my own findings?
- Have I contributed to any internal change programs?
- Do I listen to ideas for change coming from below?
- Do I react positively to demands for change?

Exercise

Complete the following chart to gain an understanding of how open you are to change within an organization.

Assessing Your Change Management Skills[1]

Instruction: Read each question and decide if this describes you and reflects your thinking and feelings. If it does completely, then it is a 4. If it does not all, then it is a 1. Respond to each question and mark whether it is a 1, 2, 3 or 4.

	Question	1	2	3	4	Comments
1	I try to anticipate and lead change within my organization.					
2	I make full use of the latest technology in my work and life.					
3	I take any changes in my context, in technology, developments in theology and education seriously.					
4	I continually look for radical as well as continual changes.					
5	I like to be different and seek productive ways of creating difference.					
6	I take an open-ended approach towards new ideas and possibilities.					
7	I link change to any known needs of churches and ministries.					
8	I keep my change philosophy simple and concise.					
9	I involve faculty, students, churches and ministries in my plans for change.					
10	I make a full and careful business case for changes and change projects.					
11	I break change projects into manageable components.					
12	I consult widely in the process of deciding on strategy and action.					

1. Adapted from Robert Heller, *Managing Change* (New York: DK Adult, 1998), 66–69.

13	I obtain people's agreements to the actions demanded of them.					
14	I use and develop teams as the basic units of change management.					
15	I use quick-fix changes for instant results early in the change program.					
16	I plan well ahead for the long-term payoff of change.					
17	I am careful not to create over-optimistic or over-pessimistic expectations.					
18	I seize opportunities to reward, celebrate and encourage successful change.					
19	I make sure everybody knows the answer to "What's in it for me?"					
20	I have effective and adaptable contingency plans available.					
21	I anticipate adverse reactions and plan how to deal with them.					
22	I use well-designed pilot projects and experiments to test my change plans.					
23	I share relevant information with colleagues and staff as soon as possible.					
24	I work closely with like-minded people who are eager to change.					
25	My own behavior is flexible and highly adaptable to changing needs.					
26	I encourage people to speak their minds openly and to air their concerns.					
27	I tackle resistance to change promptly, fairly and vigorously.					
28	I use quantitative measurement to obtain the results I want.					
29	I review and revise the assumptions that underlie the change plan.					
30	I ensure that thorough training keeps people up-to-date with change.					

31	I start the next change project as another draws to a close.					
32	I use self-appraisal to check on the organization and myself.					
	TOTAL					**TOTAL SCORE:**

Understanding Your Score

32-64 You are resisting change and are not convinced of the benefits of the changes. Overcome your fears, and learn to plan for change.

65-95 You understand the need for change – now you need to develop your skills to successfully manage it.

96-128 You are a skilled agent of change. But remember that change is a never-ending process. So expect more change

Reflection

To become effective to lead the process of change, identify the following:

- Are there personal **attitudes** I need to address in order to be an effective agent and leader of change?
- Are there things about the process of change that I need to **understand** better in order to be an effective agent and leader of change?
- Are there **skills** I need to learn and master better in order to be an effective agent and leader of change?

Appendix

Sample Toolkit

1. This is a sample set of question to either interview graduates individually or use in a focus group discussion of graduates.

OUTCOME - Graduate Feedback Interview		
Date		
Name of Graduate **Program of Study** **Year of Graduation**		
Question		**Response**
What type of ministry or ministries are they involved in? (Pastoral, Church Planting, Children and Youth Ministries) In order to have a more comprehensive understanding of their ministry: In which of the following categories are they involved and what specifically are they doing? a. Preaching b. Teaching c. Discipleship, mentoring, training d. Ministry to families/children/youth/women e. Church planting f. Counseling g. Evangelism h. Addressing social needs of the poor and marginalized (project management) i. Conflict management within the church j. Community restoration k. Church governance, structure, and leadership l. Financial management m. Ministry to the business world Scale 1–5 1: Doesn't do 3: Does sometimes 5: Does regularly		

What are two or three of the most important things they learned at the seminary? -How are they using these in their ministry? -How often? -What else from seminary are they using in their ministry? (both theological & applied learning) Scale: 1–5 1: Rarely using (annually) 3: Using sometimes (bi-monthly) 5: Using regularly (several times per month)	
What from the seminary are they not using? Scale: 1–3 1: Unrelated to their ministry 3: Directly related to their ministry (show them list of courses, ask which courses were valuable, which were not, and why.)	
What did they wish they had learned at seminary? Scale: 1–3 1: Studied, but desiring more coverage 3: Not covered in curriculum studied	
5. How well prepared did they feel at the beginning of their current position? What could the seminary do to be more effective in preparing future graduates for similar positions? Scale: 1–5 1: Completely unprepared 3: Moderately prepared 5: Extremely well prepared	
6. (If involved in a para-church organization) How do they see the relationship between their organization and the local church? Scale: 1–3 1: Unrelated 3: Intrinsically/strategically linked	

7. What are the main challenges their church/organization and community are facing right now? Have they encountered any new issues in the community? Scale: 1–5 1: Not addressing 3: Addressing somewhat; limited effectiveness 5: Addressing effectively	
8. Do they use the graduate profile? If so, how often do they reflect on where they are within that ministry roadmap? Scale: 1–5 1: Doesn't use 3: Uses rarely 5: Uses regularly	
9. In what ways did seminary affect their personal sense of calling from God? Scale: 1–5 1: Didn't affect their sense of calling 3: Moderately affected their sense of calling 5: Greatly affected their sense of calling	
Additional comments/notes:	

2. *This is a sample of questions to use when interviewing the leaders and members of the church where the graduate is ministering.*

OUTCOME – Church/Organization Focus Group – Feedback		
Date		
Name of Church/Organization		
Question		**Response**
How are the seminary graduates (and students) involved in the church/organization? (If possible, list their name, program of study, and year of graduation)		

If the church/organization were to hire a Christian worker* today, what qualities would it like them to have?
   -Attitude
   -Skills
   -Knowledge
 	
To what extent is the seminary producing Christian workers* with these qualities?	

Which of the following categories are important to the church/organization, and which ones are they engaged in? a. Preaching b. Teaching c. Discipleship, mentoring, training d. Ministry to families/children/youth/women e. Church planting f. Counseling g. Evangelism h. Addressing social needs – of the poor and marginalized (project management) i. Conflict management within the church j. Community restoration k. Church governance, structure, and leadership l. Financial management m. Ministry to the business world	
What does the church/organization governance/structure look like? Where does the Christian worker* fit within it?	
Describe the vision of the church/organization. Is there a sense that the church/organization has a common vision? In general, how can a Christian worker* enable a church/organization to accomplish its vision?	

What challenges is the church/organization facing?
   -internal
   -external	

Concluding thoughts: How can seminary be more effective in training Christian workers*?	
Additional comments/notes:	

* "Christian Worker" in this context could be identified as a Pastor, Church Planter, Minister to Children & Youth, House Church Leader, NGO worker, etc.

3. *These are sample questions that may be used when interviewing members of the community where the church is located. The purpose of these interviews is to determine how the church is perceived and the impact of the church on the community.*

IMPACT – Neighborhood Interviews		
Date		
Name of Church/Organization		
Question		**Response**
Have you heard of this church? (Name of local church where seminary graduate is serving, or the pastor's name, etc.?)		
Have you had any interaction with people from this church? (If yes, give details)		
What do you think this church believes? (Why do you think this?)		
In general, what should a church's role be in their community? What can the church and community do to improve their relationship?		
Is the church a positive or negative thing in the society? What could the church do to be a positive thing in the society?		
Do you have Christian friends? Can you describe them? What are they like?		
What do you believe about God?		
What comes to mind when you think about a) reconciliation? b) forgiveness? c) acceptance? d) justice? (or any other "Kingdom Values" talked about in the courses at seminary)		
Additional comments/notes:		

4. These are sample questions to use when visiting a church's project or ministry location to determine how the church is involved in the community.

IMPACT – Church's Community Involvement
If possible, visit some of the church's projects and ministry locations.

- A. How is the church involved with the community and society in responding to needs through service delivery, development projects and/or advocacy?
- B. How is the church integrating the good news of the kingdom of God into the demonstration of the reality of the Kingdom?

5. These are sample questions in trying to assess society's perception of basic Christian truths and trends in society.

IMPACT – Key Informant Interview
- A. Perceptions of the church and its effectiveness/impact/influence by:
  - a. Key church leaders
  - b. Outsiders/non-believers
- B. What is society's understanding of:
  - a. God (Christ, Trinity, etc.)
  - b. The Bible
  - c. The church
  - d. Salvation
- C. What competing messages are out there in society and what media are they using?

Bibliography

Banks, Robert. *Reenvisioning Theological Education*. Grand Rapids: Eerdmans, 1999.

Barth, Karl. *God in Action*. Edinburgh: T & T. Clark, 1936.

Cronshaw, Darren. "Reenvisioning Theological Education and Missional Spirituality." *Journal of Adult Theological Education* 9, no. 1 (2012): 9–27.

Edgar, Brian. "The Theology of Theological Education." *Evangelical Review of Theology* 29, no. 3 (2005): 208–217.

"Evaluation of Development Programmes: DAC Criteria for Evaluating Development Assistance," OECD better Policies for Better Life, accessed 12 July, 2014, http://www.oecd.org/development/evaluation/daccriteriaforevaluatingdevelopmentassistance.htm

Finger, Thomas N. *Contemporary Anabaptist Theology: Biblical, Historical, Constructive*. Downers Grove: InterVarsity Press, 2004.

Franke, John. *The Character of Theology: An Introduction to Its Nature, Task, and Purpose*. Grand Rapids: Baker Academic, 2005.

Frei, Hans W. *Types of Christian Theology*. eds. George Hunsinger and William C. Plancher. New Haven: Yale University Press, 1992.

Grenz, Stanley and Roger Olson. *Who Needs Theology? An Invitation to the Study of God*. Downers Grove: InterVarsity Press, 1996.

Hall, Douglas John. *The Cross in Our Context: Jesus and the Suffering World*. Minneapolis: Fortress Press, 2003.

Heibert, Paul. *Anthropological Reflections on Missiological Issues*. Grand Rapids: Baker, 1994.

Heller, Robert, *Managing Change*. New York: DK Adult, 1998, 66–69.

Jaeger, Werner. *Early Christianity and Greek paideia*. Cambridge: Harvard University Press, 1961.

Joughin, Gordon, and Ranald MacDonald. "A Model of Assessment in Higher Education Institutions." The Higher Education Academy. Accessed 12 September 2014. https://www.llas.ac.uk/resourcedownloads/2968/Joughin_and_Macdonald_model_assessment.pdf

Kelsey, David H. *Between Athens and Berlin: The Theological Debate*. Grand Rapids: Eerdmans, 1993.

Kertesi, Gabor. "The Assessment and Evaluation of Educational Institutions, School Accountability." In *Green Book for the Renewal of Public Education in Hungary,* edited by Janos Kollo and Julia Varga, 179–200. Budapest: Ecostat Government Institute for Strategic Research of Economy and Society, 2009.

Lehtonen, Teemu J. "Leadership Formation in the Global Context." DMin diss., Acadia Divinity College, Acadia University, 2014.

McClendon, Jr., James Wm. *Systematic Theology: Doctrine, Vol. 2.* Nashville: Abingdon Press, 1994.

McClendon, James. *Ethics: Systematic Theology Vol. 1.* Nashville: Abingdon Press, 2002.

McGrath, Alister E. *Christian Theology: An Introduction,* 5th. Chichester: Wiley-Blackwell, 2011.

Migliore, Daniel. *Faith Seeking Understanding: An Introduction to Christian Theology.* Grand Rapids: Eerdmans, 2004.

Murray, Stuart. *Church After Christendom.* Bletchley: Paternoster, 2005.

Newbigin, Lesslie. *Sign of the Kingdom.* Grand Rapids: Eerdmans, 1981.

Niebuhr, H. Richard. *Christ and Culture.* New York: Harper, 1951.

Peterson, Eugene. *Under the Unpredictable Plant: An Exploration in Vocational Holiness.* Grand Rapids: Eerdmans, 1994.

Schleiermacher, Friedrich and Terrence Tice. *Brief Outline of Theology as a Field of Study: Revised Translation of the 1811 and 1830 Editions,* 3rd ed. Louisville: Westminster John Knox Press, 2011.

Taleb, Nassim Nicholas. *The Black Swan: The Impact of the Highly Improbable.* New York: Random House Trade Paperbacks, 2010.

Tarnas, Richard. *The Passion of the Western Mind: Understanding the Ideas that have Shaped our World View.* New York: Harmony Books, 1993.

Verhoeven, Jef C. "Assessment and Management in Institutions of Higher Education." In *Quality Assessment for Higher Education in Europe,* edited by Alessandro Cavalli, 27–41. Pavia: Portland Press Ltd., 2007.

Percy, Walker. In *Conversations with Walker Percy,* edited by Peggy Whitman Prenshaw. Jackson: University of Mississippi Press, 1985.

Wood, Charles. *Vision and Discernment: An Orientation in Theological Studies.* Atlanta: Scholars Press, 1985.

ICETE International Council for Evangelical Theological Education
strengthening evangelical theological education through international cooperation

ICETE is a global community, sponsored by nine regional associations of theological schools, to enable international interaction and collaboration among all those concerned for the enhancement of evangelical theological education worldwide.

The purpose of ICETE is:
1. To promote the enhancement of evangelical theological education worldwide.
2. To serve as a forum for contact and collaboration among those worldwide involved in evangelical theological education, for mutual assistance, stimulation and enrichment.
3. To provide networking and support services for regional associations of evangelical theological schools worldwide.
4. To facilitate among these bodies the enhancement of their services to evangelical theological education within their regions.

Sponsoring associations include:

Africa: Association for Christian Theological Education in Africa (ACTEA)

Asia: Asia Theological Association (ATA)

Caribbean: Caribbean Evangelical Theological Association (CETA)

Europe: European Evangelical Accrediting Association (EEAA)

Euro-Asia: Euro-Asian Accrediting Association (E-AAA)

Latin America: Association for Evangelical Theological Education in Latin America (AETAL)

Middle East and North Africa: Middle East Association for Theological Education (MEATE)

North America: Association for Biblical Higher Education (ABHE)

South Pacific: South Pacific Association of Evangelical Colleges (SPAEC)

www.icete-edu.org

Langham Literature and its imprints are a ministry of Langham Partnership.

Langham Partnership is a global fellowship working in pursuit of the vision God entrusted to its founder John Stott –

> *to facilitate the growth of the church in maturity and Christ-likeness through raising the standards of biblical preaching and teaching.*

Our vision is to see churches in the majority world equipped for mission and growing to maturity in Christ through the ministry of pastors and leaders who believe, teach and live by the Word of God.

Our mission is to strengthen the ministry of the Word of God through:
- nurturing national movements for biblical preaching
- fostering the creation and distribution of evangelical literature
- enhancing evangelical theological education

especially in countries where churches are under-resourced.

Our ministry

Langham Preaching partners with national leaders to nurture indigenous biblical preaching movements for pastors and lay preachers all around the world. With the support of a team of trainers from many countries, a multi-level programme of seminars provides practical training, and is followed by a programme for training local facilitators. Local preachers' groups and national and regional networks ensure continuity and ongoing development, seeking to build vigorous movements committed to Bible exposition.

Langham Literature provides majority world pastors, scholars and seminary libraries with evangelical books and electronic resources through grants, discounts and distribution. The programme also fosters the creation of indigenous evangelical books for pastors in many languages, through training workshops for writers and editors, sponsored writing, translation, strengthening local evangelical publishing houses, and investment in major regional literature projects, such as one volume Bible commentaries like *The Africa Bible Commentary*.

Langham Scholars provides financial support for evangelical doctoral students from the majority world so that, when they return home, they may train pastors and other Christian leaders with sound, biblical and theological teaching. This programme equips those who equip others. Langham Scholars also works in partnership with majority world seminaries in strengthening evangelical theological education. A growing number of Langham Scholars study in high quality doctoral programmes in the majority world itself. As well as teaching the next generation of pastors, graduated Langham Scholars exercise significant influence through their writing and leadership.

To learn more about Langham Partnership and the work we do visit **langham.org**

CPSIA information can be obtained
at www.ICGtesting.com
Printed in the USA
BVHW042055051121
620926BV00008B/92

9 781783 680689